TOP TEAMS IN WOMEN'S SOCCER

WOMEN'S SOCCER TODAY

Superstars of Women's Soccer

Top Teams in Women's Soccer

U.S. Women's Team

Women's Soccer on the Rise

TOP TEAMS
IN WOMEN'S
SOCCER

BRYCE KANE

MASON CREST

Mason Crest
450 Parkway Drive, Suite D
Broomall, Pennsylvania 19008
(866) MCP-BOOK (toll free)

First printing
9 8 7 6 5 4 3 2 1

ISBN (hardback) 978-1-4222-4214-8
ISBN (series) 978-1-4222-4212-4
ISBN (ebook) 978-1-4222-7596-2

Library of Congress Cataloging-in-Publication Data on file

Developed and Produced by National Highlights Inc.
Editor: Andrew Luke
Interior and cover design: Annalisa Gumbrecht, Studio Gumbrecht
Production: Michelle Luke

QR CODES AND LINKS TO THIRD-PARTY CONTENT

CONTENTS

Chapter 1   USA.. 7

Chapter 2   Germany... 23

Chapter 3   Japan 37

Chapter 4   Norway.. 49

Chapter 5   Best of the Rest.. 63

            Glossary of Soccer Terms... 76

            Further Reading, Internet Resources.............................. 77

            Index 78

            Author's Biography and Credits..................................... 80

KEY ICONS TO LOOK FOR:

 WORDS TO UNDERSTAND: These words with their easy-to-understand definitions will increase the reader's understanding of the text while building vocabulary skills.

 SIDEBARS: This boxed material within the main text allows readers to build knowledge, gain insights, explore possibilities, and broaden their perspectives by weaving together additional information to provide realistic and holistic perspectives.

 EDUCATIONAL VIDEOS: Readers can view videos by scanning our QR codes, providing them with additional educational content to supplement the text. Examples include news coverage, moments in history, speeches, iconic sports moments, and much more!

 TEXT-DEPENDENT QUESTIONS: These questions send the reader back to the text for more careful attention to the evidence presented there.

 RESEARCH PROJECTS: Readers are pointed toward areas of further inquiry connected to each chapter. Suggestions are provided for projects that encourage deeper research and analysis.

 WORDS TO UNDERSTAND

caps
international tournaments a player has competed in

despondency
the state of being extremely low in spirits

magnified
enlarged, intensified

minuscule
extremely small; tiny

CHAPTER 1

USA

Few teams in FIFA Women's World Cup history have had as much continual success as the United States Women's National Team (USWNT). Unlike the men's team, which has yet to rise to the top ranks of the sport, the women's team has been successful from the very beginning. The USWNT was the first champion in the event's history in 1991, winning six matches out of six and outscoring opponents 25–5.

The United States then won a second title in 1999 by winning five matches and tying one while outscoring opponents 18–3. The most recent USWNT championship win was in the 2015 event, where it won six games, tied one, and outscored opponents 14–3. These were not just occasional bright spots in an otherwise lackluster history. The USWNT has finished in the top three in every World Cup and is almost always considered one of the best teams in the event. A combination of dedication and skilled youth development leagues has made the United States the best women's soccer team for decades.

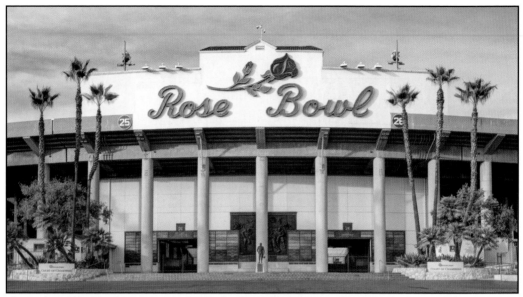

The Rose Bowl in Pasadena, CA, was the site for the 1999 FIFA Women's World Cup final match.

THE BEST MOMENTS IN USWNT HISTORY

THE 1999 CHAMPIONSHIP RUN

Undoubtedly the most significant moment in USWNT history was when they won the 1999 FIFA Women's World Cup championship. They were not only considered one of the best teams in the world at the time, but also were playing on American soil in eight different stadiums, including legendary venues such as the Rose Bowl in Los Angeles and Soldier Field in Chicago.

Going home with anything less than the title would have caused **despondency** for American fans, which made up the majority of the nearly 1.2 million people who attended the event. The earliest USWNT matches in the event were exciting, as the Americans came out of the group stage winning all three matches with a favorable goal ratio of 13:1. Their domination made it very easy to advance to the knockout stage.

However, the knockout stage was a bit tougher for the USWNT. On July 1, they won 3–2 over Germany in the quarterfinals in Landover, Maryland The match started out rough for the United States as American defender Brandi Chastain scored an own-goal five minutes in to give Germany a 1–0 lead. That kind of mistake has cost teams the win many times.

However, America's Tiffeny Milbrett tied it up in the sixteenth minute to make things more interesting. The score remained tied until Germany took a 2–1 lead just before halftime on a goal from Bettina Wiegmann. Chastain redeemed herself with a goal just four minutes into the second half to tie it up, while Joy Fawcett scored the eventual match winner in the sixty-sixth minute.

Brandi Chastain's World Cup winning celebration is one of the greatest moments in USWNT history and in all of women's sports.

The semifinal match was much less tense as America celebrated a 2–0 blanking of Brazil that set up the final against China at the Rose Bowl. This match took place in temperatures of more than 100ºF (37.8ºC) and was an exhilarating match that saw full time end with a 0–0 draw. After two extra-time halves without a score, the U.S. won 5–4 on penalty kicks.

The big break in the shoot-out undoubtedly came when Briana Scurry, the United States goalkeeper, stopped Liu Ying's third round attempt. This save set up a 4–4 score, with Brandi Chastain taking the final kick. Her shot went past the outstretched hands of Gao Hong to bring America its second World Cup victory and its first on American soil.

After scoring the goal, Chastain famously fell to her knees and tore off her jersey in celebration. This celebratory gesture was immortalized on numerous magazine covers and caused a minor controversy in the United States, as this move revealed her sports bra, which would not raise an eyebrow today. In response to the debate over the propriety of her gesture, Chastain stated that the celebration was "momentary insanity" in celebration of "the greatest moment of my life on the soccer field."

THE BIG COMEBACK IN 2015

The 2015 FIFA Women's World Cup was a make-or-break moment for the USWNT. Their reputation as the best women's soccer team in the world was in jeopardy because they hadn't won a championship in the World Cup since 1999. Since then, they had third place finishes in 2003 and 2007, and a second place finish in 2011. As a result, they wanted to come out with a win in this tournament to show that they were still the team to beat.

The intensity of the situation was only magnified by the fact that they were set up to play Japan in the final, the team that had defeated them in the 2011 championship match in a penalty kick shoot-out win. As a result, they felt pressure in the tournament that hadn't been there in the last sixteen years. They negotiated the three matches in group D, winning 3–1 against Australia, drawing 0–0 with Sweden, and beating Nigeria 1–0 to advance.

That lone goal scored by Australia was the only one America gave up until the final against Japan. In fact, many experts claim that the United States couldn't have won without keeper Hope Solo. During the tournament, she put on an athletic performance that is likely one of the best in World Cup history. In seven matches, she gave up just three goals and held her opponents scoreless for a Women's World Cup record 540 consecutive minutes.

In fact, the only goal she truly gave up during the final was a beautiful shot from Japan's Yūki Nagasato in the twenty-seventh minute. The second goal for Japan was a blooper own-goal that happened in the fifty-second minute when a shot unexpectedly bounced off the head of American defender Julie Johnston. This deflection took Solo by surprise and snuck past her when the ball changed direction.

Solo's efforts earned her the coveted Golden Glove award, which is given to the tournament's best goalkeeper. This award was gratifying for the keeper, as Solo had nearly been left off the team entirely following a run-in with the law and a thirty-day suspension from U.S. Soccer just six months prior to the tournament.

The final game did not disappoint U.S. fans, as the team went on to win 5–2 in a near-blowout game. Beyond Solo and her critical saves, Carli Lloyd was also crucial to the win. She scored a hat trick by netting goals in the third, fifth, and sixteenth minutes of the game. This made Lloyd not only the first woman to score a hat trick in the World Cup final, but also the player to do it the quickest, either male or female.

Just days after winning the 2015 FIFA World Cup and the Golden Glove award for best goalkeeper, Hope Solo attended the ESPY awards, where the USWB+NT won for Best Team.

FROM STARTER TO BACKUP TO STARTER AGAIN

Though Carli Lloyd was the hero of the 2015 FIFA Women's World Cup final, she had to travel a long way to reach that point. At thirty-two, she was getting to the age when many players consider retiring. In fact, she considered it in 2012 during that year's Olympic games, when she was placed in a backup role. This heartbreaking moment caused Lloyd to debate her skills and to wonder if her peak had passed. However, she proved those fears unfounded when she was returned to the starting lineup in time for the gold-medal match against Japan. In that match, she rewarded fans and supporters by scoring both of the team's goals to give America a record four gold medals.

BEST USA PLAYERS EVER

ABBY WAMBACH

After Hamm's retirement, Abby Wambach was the most dominant player in women's soccer. Her statistics through a career that ended in 2015 are staggering. For example, Wambach shattered Hamm's USWNT career goal record by scoring 184 international goals, which is by far the top total for either men or women.

Abby Wambach celebrates the USWNT victory in the 2015 FIFA Women's World Cup at a parade in New York City.

Wambach won two Olympic gold medals and scored the gold-medal-winning goal in the 2004 games. And in 2011, she scored a blazing equalizer in the FIFA Women's World Cup quarterfinal against Brazil. This win not only helped the team advance to the finals, but also returned them to global prominence. In 2015, she finally achieved her lifelong goal of winning the FIFA Women's World Cup championship.

When Wambach retired in 2015, she had scored the seventh-most career goals by way of the header, with seventy-seven goals. Her dynamic flair for the header made her one of its best users. For example, Wambach's 2004 gold-medal-winning goal was a header, as was her goal against Brazil in the 2011 World Cup. Few players are able to score so often in such a dramatic way.

Mia Hamm averaged an assist at least every other match—a USWNT record.

MIA HAMM

Mia Hamm is one of the most unlikely soccer superstars of all time. Known to be a very introverted woman, she was nonetheless considered the Michael Jordan of the sport. That honor was due not only to Hamm's scoring abilities, but also to her influence on popularizing the game in her home country.

In college, Hamm led UNC to four straight NCAA championships and a 94–1 record. She then made headlines by debuting with the 1991 World Cup team at the age of nineteen. Hamm's success in this tournament started early, as she scored in the first match of the competition. With her steady presence and mature personality, she and Akers were able to lead the team to FIFA Women's World Cup championships in 1991 and 1999.

Due to her girl-next-door personality and raw scoring ability, Hamm was one of the few female soccer players to earn marketing deals, including long-term agreements with Nike and Gatorade. Along with

Akers, she was vital in helping to win America's Olympic gold medals in 1996 and 2004. Hamm's scoring feats include 158 career goals and a record 145 assists.

MICHELLE AKERS

Akers has been called the "Babe Ruth of women's soccer," and her success was due to a unique combination of energy, skill, and dominating size. At nearly 6 feet (1.8 meters) tall, she was one of the tallest and most intimidating players of her time.

Akers was part of the dominant 1991 U.S. Women's World Cup championship team and was an amazing player that year. For example, she scored thirty-nine goals in twenty-six matches, a rate of 1.5 goals per game. Her skills were crucial in getting America qualified for the first World Cup, as she scored eleven goals to get her team into the tournament.

Akers then scored eight times in the World Cup to lead the team to the final match against Norway. It was there that Akers sealed her legendary status by scoring two more goals in the 2–1 win. Her second goal was the true stunner of the competition, as Akers put it into the net with just two minutes left in the match.

Despite Akers having to fight chronic fatigue syndrome since 1994, she remained a crucial player for the U.S. Women's team and its continued dominance of the sport. In the 1999 World Cup tournament, she nailed a late penalty kick during the semifinal game to advance past Brazil. For her efforts, she won the Bronze Ball as the tournament's third best player. Akers retired in 2000.

Akers was given the Order of Merit honor by FIFA in 1998 and was named to the National Soccer Hall of Fame in 2002. In 2004, she was named one of the 125 greatest living soccer players by FIFA.

YOUTH DEVELOPMENT PROGRAMS ARE BIG IN AMERICA

Such sustained success by the U.S. Women's National Soccer Team has been possible thanks to the growth of youth programs throughout the nation. While the sport is not as prevalent in America as it is throughout the rest of the world, that hasn't stopped great programs from flourishing. U.S. Soccer is the governing body of soccer in the United States and has been in operation for more than 100 years.

The USWNT continues to have skilled players to choose from due to the strength of youth development programs in the girl's game.

During that time, it has focused heavily on developing both the men's and women's national teams. U.S. Soccer was critical in helping the men's team improve from the laughingstock they were for nearly forty years into a competitive and respected team. From 1990 to 2014, the men competed in seven straight FIFA World Cup tournaments and got as far as the quarterfinals in 2002. While they didn't qualify for the 2018 tournament, the increased focus on youth leagues is likely to make the men's team a tough challenger in future events.

On that note, one of the biggest reasons for the USWNT's continued dominance is the dedication of American soccer programs to developing talent at a young age. Many of the best female players rise through the ranks of U.S. Youth Soccer and the American

Youth Soccer Organization (AYSO). These groups are dedicated to identifying high-quality players, analyzing their abilities, and helping them become more successful and competitive.

HOW YOUTH SOCCER HELPS

U.S. Youth Soccer and AYSO are dedicated to the development of players aged four to nineteen. These are primarily educational groups that work to instill in each player a love and dedication for soccer. They avoid the "win at all costs" mentality that often turns many players off of sports. Instead, they focus on making it a fun experience that all players can enjoy.

Another aspect of their mission is to teach young players about the importance of teamwork and knowing that personal playing time is not as important as team success and having a good time. By making the sport as fun as possible, these groups hope to inspire a lifelong love of soccer that encourages female players to compete at higher levels, and to expand and enhance the professional experience.

Developmental programs exist that meet the needs of players at all skill levels.

Each of their programs is fine-tuned to meet the needs of developing players at every level. For example, some programs are designed specifically to help less skilled players enhance their abilities. However, elite programs are offered that identify the best youth female soccer players in the nation and work on providing them with the ability to earn college scholarships. They also teach them how to prepare for Olympic and national team tryouts.

THE ELITE CLUBS

The Elite Clubs National League was founded in 2009 and is dedicated to identifying standout youth female soccer players and improving their abilities. The Elite Clubs' role is to streamline the process of finding the best female soccer players and getting them on the right teams for their continued development.

For example, they have worked to improve the process of identifying elite players and getting them on the U.S. Youth Soccer national teams. They work heavily on scouting and identification programs and teach scouts how to spot genuinely dominant players. Beyond this, they also focus on daily training programs that improve the skills of female soccer players.

Take a look at the host cities for the 2019 Women's World Cup tournament in France

While the Elite Clubs program is still in its earliest stages, it showcases just how vital youth competition is for the development of excellent female players. And while America's attention to female soccer may be limited to only World Cup and Olympic years at the moment, continued USWNT dominance may inspire even more players to join these youth leagues.

WILL THEY WIN IT ALL?

It's hard to imagine the USWNT not coming away with their fourth championship win in 2019—it was ranked number one in the world through 2018. In an effort to maintain their superiority, the Americans reshuffled the team to focus on younger players. While this move has frustrated a few of the veteran players on the team, it is an inevitable part of maintaining success and dominance.

The USWNT is used to winning, as seen here at the 2022 CONCACAF Olympic qualifying tournament. Nothing short of victory will be expected of the team at the 2019 FIFA Women's World Cup.

While championship winners like Carli Lloyd are still on the team and will play a critical part, younger and perhaps less experienced players are being brought up to compete for key spots. Expect players like Morgan Brian, who was the youngest player on the 2015 U.S. Women's National Team, to fight for room against newer players like Rose Lavelle and Samantha Mewis.

Lavelle is just twenty-three years old and plays with the Washington Spirit in the National Women's Soccer League (NWSL). While she has had successes, including being named the Big Ten Freshman of the Year and being selected first overall in the 2017 NWSL draft, her experience on such a large and global stage is relatively **minuscule**, with fewer than twenty **caps** going into 2019.

Twenty-five-year-old Mewis was a reliable player for the Western New York Flash and then the rebranded North Carolina Courage (she scores a goal about every four matches), and she is expected to be a significant contributor to the 2019 FIFA Women's World Cup team. It is critical to develop younger talent in such big tournaments, however, as it is the only way to replace aging players who may no longer be at the peak of their abilities.

PLAYERS WHO ARE LIKELY TO MAKE AN IMPACT

Let's start by taking a look at who is likely to make an impact at the goalkeeper position in 2019. Alyssa Naeher is coach Jill Ellis' starter, with more than thirty caps going into 2019. However, expect U-19 Women's World Cup champion Ashlyn Harris to push for playing time if Naeher falters.

Defenders who will keep America competitive in 2019 include co-captain Becky Sauerbrunn, one of the most experienced players on the team. She already has more than 140 caps and is likely to help promising young players like twenty-six-year-old Abby Dahlkemper and twenty-year-old Tierna Davidson learn how to compete at a high level.

Co-captain Carli Lloyd, who has more than 250 caps and more than 100 goals in international tournaments, is likely to lead the midfielders. While her 2015 FIFA Women's World Cup final-match hat trick is likely the best moment in her career so far, adding a career-crowning second World Cup would be another high point. Other midfielders to watch include Morgan Brian and Lindsey Horan, USWNT veterans at just twenty-six and twenty-five years old respectively.

Alex Morgan will be expected to do what she does best – terrorize opposing goalkeepers.

And finally, we come to the forwards. Expect co-captain Alex Morgan to continue showcasing her excellent skills this year. Closing in on 150 caps and 100 goals entering 2019, she remains a dominant player. Other players to watch include veterans Christen Press and Megan Rapinoe, both with more than 100 caps.

WHAT IT WILL TAKE FOR AMERICA TO WIN AGAIN

If the United States. wins the 2019 FIFA Women's World Cup, it will not only log a fourth championship, but will also be just the second team to win back-to-back championships. The last time that happened was in 2003 and 2007 when Germany took home the title in both tournaments. No other side has experienced that kind of success, and if America wins, they will match a hard-to-reach precedent.

However, there are a few problems that could hold the U.S. team back. First of all, it is going to have a huge target painted on its back. Teams that may otherwise have been minimally competitive are likely to come at them as hard as they can. Everybody wants to be the team to beat the Americans, and if a team were somehow able to get them knocked out of the group stage, they'd be legendary in their home country.

That problem is less of an issue than the relative youth of many of the up-and-coming players. In 2015, a number of high-quality team members reached their peak or ended their careers on a strong note. For example, goalkeeper Hope Solo retired, and replacing a player who had such a monumental impact on a team is very difficult.

All that said, the United States remains the front-runner for the 2019 FIFA Women's World Cup championship. Even though the players are relatively young and inexperienced, they are still the number one team in the world. That speaks volumes about the talent on their squad.

TEXT-DEPENDENT QUESTIONS:

1. Who scored the hat trick for the USWNT in the 2015 FIFA Women's World Cup final against Japan?

2. Name two youth soccer associations dedicated to making the game more fun.

3. Which player scored the winning shoot-out goal in 1999 and was later criticized for her celebration?

RESEARCH PROJECT:

Talk to several youth soccer leagues and learn more about how they identify high-quality players. Identify a player at a high school or college and track her progress through a season in one of these programs. Chart this information to showcase the success of youth training programs.

 WORDS TO UNDERSTAND

equalizer
a goal that ties the score of a contest

fostering
promoting the growth or development of someone
or something

immersive
providing, involving, or characterized by deep
absorption in something

sexism
prejudice or discrimination based on gender

CHAPTER 2

Germany

The German men's national soccer team is one of the best and most successful teams of all time. And while the German women's soccer team has won two World Cup titles of its own, it wasn't initially so successful. In fact, women's soccer was considered by the country to be an embarrassment for years, not due to its lack of success, but by merely existing.

In fact, the team's 1989 European Championship victory may have been both the team's most significant success at the time and its most embarrassing. That's because the players were given nothing more than a tea set for their win (yes, actual cups and saucers), an issue that raised accusations of **sexism** within the sport. Thankfully, that problem has improved considerably over the years. Women are still fighting for fair and equal treatment across the sport, but many teams now receive cash payments for competing and cash bonuses for winning.

The fight for acceptance in their home country is, perhaps, why the German team has become one of the most respected in World Cup history. While the back-to-back championships in 2003 and 2007 (the only time that has happened in Women's World Cup history) have yet to be matched, they have also finished in second place once and in fourth place twice.

GERMANY'S GREATEST SUCCESSES

THE BREAKTHROUGH IN 2003

While Germany has been a successful team in recent World Cup tournaments, 2003 was its biggest year. The Germans had several skilled players and were poised to bring home the title from the 2003 tournament. In the group stage, they started out very strongly. Their wins included a 4–1 rout of Canada, a 3–0 blanking of Japan, and a 6–1 blowout of Argentina for goal totals of 13–2.

Germany defeated Sweden 2-1 in the final match of the 2003 FIFA Women's World Cup to win its first ever Women's World Cup title.

The knockout stage was just as easy for the team to dominate. Germany blazed past Russia 7–1 in the quarterfinals and stunned the defending U.S. champs with a 3–0 blanking in the semifinals. The Germans then went on to pull off a 2–1 win over Sweden, a defense-oriented team that had surrendered just five goals in five matches coming into the final.

This victory did not come easily for the German team, which had beaten every previous opponent in the tournament by at least three goals. Birgit Prinz, who went on to win the Golden Ball as the best player in the tournament, was unable to score, shut down by Sweden's smothering defense. As a result, Sweden was able to get a lead when Hanna Ljungberg scored in the forty-first minute.

However, Maren Meinert scored the **equalizer** to open the second half to keep Germany in the match. In fact, that goal was the last one earned in regulation time, as Germany and Sweden gave each other few chances to score.

In extra time, things stayed even until Nia Künzer blasted a goal into the net in the ninety-eighth minute, and Germany held on for the win. Prinz won awards as both top scorer and best player in the tournament. The long road to World Cup glory had been well paved at this point and the Germans made no mistake in laying claim to their first title.

Now a soccer commentator for German TV, Nia Künzer scored the World Cup winning goal for Germany in 2003.

THE EPIC SECOND WIN IN 2007

When the 2007 FIFA Women's World Cup rolled around, Germany was still the team to beat. While the American team is almost always considered the favorite to win, lots of people were putting their money on the Germans to repeat. There were good reasons for that confidence. The team included many of the same key players from 2003 and was poised for more success.

Watch the highlights of Germany's second straight World Cup final win

Germany showed off its dominance early in the group stages by trouncing Argentina with a shocking 11–0 score. They then drew with England before ensuring an advance with a 2–0 win over Japan. Their plus-thirteen goal differential in the group stage is one of the largest of all time.

The team then went on to do something never before done: blank every opponent. That's right—Germany never once gave up a goal during the tournament. It owed that success to Nadine Angerer, the starting keeper for Germany for the entire tournament. Her skills and incredible saves gave her a record 540 consecutive score-free minutes, one that is likely never to be beaten.

These wins included a 3–0 quarterfinal victory over the surprising North Korean team, who earned the best showing yet for their country. The Germans then went on to beat Norway 3–0 in the semifinals and Brazil 2–0 in the finals. With this victory, Germany became the only team besides the United States to win more than one championship, and the only team to win the trophy back-to-back. In spite of the win, Germany earned only a Silver Ball award for Prinz's performance, with Marta of Brazil getting the Golden Ball.

German keeper Nadine Angerer posted an unmatched clean sheet for the entire tournament in 2007.

Nadine Angerer made the all-star team for goalkeepers. Other all-star German players included defenders Ariane Hingst and Kerstin Stegemann, midfielder Renate Lingor, and Birgit Prinz at forward.

WHAT MAKES A GREAT GOALKEEPER

Nadine Angerer's legendary performance in the 2007 FIFA Women's World Cup emphasized the attributes that make a great goalkeeper. Concentration and awareness are critical, and Angerer rarely let either lapse during the tournament. Without an understanding of the position of every player on the field and the ability to track threatening players, a goalkeeper will fail. The positioning of the keeper is also essential, as they need to follow the action of the match and get into the best spot to attempt a save. Leadership and confidence are also critical traits, all of which made Angerer the best player at her position for Germany.

GERMANY'S BEST PLAYERS EVER

BIRGIT PRINZ

Birgit Prinz is one of Germany's most important and successful female soccer players of all time. In fact, she is the highest-scoring non-North American player in the history of the sport. She scored 128 goals in just 214 matches. It should be no surprise that she was named the FIFA Women's World Player of the Year three times. Prinz also has three Olympic bronze medals (2000, 2004, and 2008) to go along with back-to-back World Cup titles and the 2003 World Cup Golden Ball.

Adored by her German fans, Prinz was named FIFA Women's World Player of the Year for three straight years, from 2003 to 2005.

Prinz was first and foremost a goal scorer. On the list of all-time leading goal scorers in the history of the FIFA Women's World Cup, she places second, having netted fourteen total goals while winning the Golden Boot in 2003. Prinz led the Frauen-Bundesliga, Germany's top women's club league, in goals four times.

All of these successes were foreseeable for Prinz, who debuted with the German national team in 1994 at just sixteen years old. She scored the game-winning goal just one minute before the end of that first match. Her skills drove team success, as she led clubs to seven league titles, eight national titles, and three UEFA Cup championships. Prinz retired in 2011, and all German players are measured against her lofty legacy.

NADINE ANGERER

Any player who records even a single World Cup shutout has achieved a noteworthy accomplishment. Someone who does it for 540 minutes in a row is an instant legend. While Angerer's success has never again reached the heady levels of the 2007 FIFA Women's World Cup, she has remained a dominant and skilled goalkeeper who rarely lets a ball slip past her fingers. In fact, her large frame and athletic performances alone earn her a spot on this list.

Teammates and coaches have praised her as a leader and a role model for her team. For example, the late Tony DiCicco, former USWNT coach, had nothing but good things to say about her after seeing her compete in the 2013 European Championship, in which Angerer played a crucial part for Germany's eventual win. He said that Angerer was not only a great teammate and leader, but also that she didn't have "any glaring weaknesses" in her game. Angerer's time with the German national team continued to be a success through her retirement in 2015, though Germany has yet to repeat the dominance of the 2007 season.

Nadine Angerer leads her Germany teammates to the field during the 2015 Algarve Cup in Portugal.

Anybody who could stop a penalty shot from Marta, however (as Angerer did in the 2007 championship win over Brazil), deserves to be on a list of great German players.

HEIDI MOHR

As prolific a scorer as Prinz was, no German woman filled the net with the same frequency as Heidi Mohr. A threat to shoot with either foot, Mohr terrorized goalkeepers in German leagues, including the Frauen-Bundesliga, for fifteen seasons. She also led the Frauen-Bundesliga in scoring for a record five straight years.

Mohr started her senior club career with TuS Niederkirchen in 1986. With this club she scored an astounding 114 goals in just eighty-three matches. She debuted for the German national team that same year at just nineteen years old. While wearing her country's colors, Mohr scored 83 times in 104 caps. That is 0.8 goals per match, significantly better than Prinz's 0.6 goals per match for Germany.

Unlike Prinz, Mohr was never able to lead her team to a FIFA Women's World Cup title. It was not for a lack of effort on Mohr's part. In 1991, she won the Silver Boot for scoring seven times in the tournament en route to a semifinal loss to the USA. In 1995, Mohr and Germany went all the way to the final before losing 2–0 to Norway.

In 1999, the Swiss-based organization the International Federation of Football History & Statistics (IFFHS) awarded Mohr the award for Female European Player of the Century.

INVESTING IN YOUTH

Soccer has been the national sport of Germany for more than 100 years, which is at the root of why they are so dominant in just about every World Cup. Even if the women's team has yet to achieve the same level of success that the men's team has enjoyed, they are still one of the top teams in the world. That success all begins with its youth programs.

In Germany, youth player development is well funded from very young ages.

In fact, it is hard to find a country that invests more money in youth soccer than Germany. Since 2001, they have spent well over $1 billion on youth player development in Germany. This includes professional youth academies, full-time coaches, and scouts working to identify high-quality players and implementing a system to develop their skills in a variety of different ways.

There are also private organizations, like GFL Soccer, that utilize a large number of soccer camps, tournaments, and more to help teach players the German style of play. During these camps, players are typically placed in an immersive environment that includes six to eight hours of soccer practice and drills every day. For female soccer players, these camps generally are the only way for them to achieve much success before they reach the high school level.

That's because girl's programs are often limited at the youth level, with most female-only teams starting for players around the age of fifteen. There usually aren't enough girls interested in playing before that age to sustain the same kind of program that the boys have. As a result, girls who are interested in soccer usually have to compete alongside boys and deal with their rougher style of play. That means that there are typically fewer girls than boys in these youth programs. One German coach estimated that there were nearly 1.5 million boys in these programs, compared to just 30,000 girls.

However, girls are accepted into these programs if they are skilled enough to compete with the boys. Most of these programs start when the child is about six years old and use an intensive system that streamlines the process and makes it easier to create great players. Currently, there are more than 10,000 teams total across multiple age levels in Germany, meaning that the level of competition is very high, even for the girls.

Even more impressively, intensive summer soccer camps are often a regular occurrence for anyone who wants to play soccer as a young person. For example, the German International ID Camp takes place for three days every summer and is a partnership between AYSES and Schächter Management Sports. AYSES, or Advanced Youth Soccer Educational System, is a developmental youth soccer program out of Texas. Schächter Management Sports is a German group that advocates for better soccer programs around the world. This camp is set up to identify high-quality players and to focus on getting them the training they need to succeed.

German soccer camps are set up to identify and nurture players with superior skills.

For example, a youth player who is skilled at a position will be sorted into an appropriate camp to foster his or her skills even further. There is also an International ID Camp that lets young people from all over the world come and compete for a spot on a German development team.

During these camps, the top fifteen players are chosen to participate in a tournament that is attended by soccer scouts from across Europe. Players can then be spotted by these professionals and get put into professional development camps, and even on teams. Here they can spend time fostering their skills and learning how to be more dominant players.

This structure of youth support makes Germany a tough team to beat, both on the men's and women's level. While a separate program for female soccer players at the youth level would increase their abilities even further, there is at least a support system that helps to create high-quality players at many levels. All of these benefits have made it possible for Germany to remain favorites in just about every World Cup.

WILL THEY WIN IT ALL?

Germany's chances of winning the FIFA Women's World Cup are always interesting to examine. While its dominance in the 2003 and 2007 championships made the Germans an impressive team to watch, its success since then has been more limited. That's partially because so many of their great players retired after that 2007 win and left them in a tough rebuilding situation.

That said, Germany is in the spot America would like to be in soon: just about wholly rebuilt. That's because the young players that Germany debuted in the 2011 and 2015 tournaments have gotten a lot more experience under their belts and are helping their team to quickly become one of the most dominant teams in the world again. In fact, they might be the real favorite to win this tournament, due to America's relative youth.

For example, let's take a look at how they did during the last World Cup tournament to get a feel for what to expect. Germany finished the group stage with a 15–1 goal record with two wins and a draw to their name. Most of these goals were scored against Ivory Coast, which Germany blew past 10–0 in the first match.

They then tied 1–1 with Norway, who is always a tough opponent, before blanking Thailand 4–0. After that, they beat Sweden 4–1 in the round of sixteen and France in the quarterfinals in a 5–4 penalty kick shoot-out following extra time. They then met the United States in the semifinals and were blanked 2–0.

After this frustrating loss, they faced England in the third place match. There they lost 1–0 to get a fourth place finish. Before meeting the United States, they had scored at least one goal in every match and looked like they could win the whole tournament. While this kind of disappointing finish is always possible even for the best team, it's doubtful Germany will do worse than they did in 2015.

In fact, Germany looked incredibly impressive during their qualifying run to the 2019 tournament, as it scored thirty eight goals during its qualifying matches and gave up just three. No other European team scored more goals in qualifying. While it is fair to say that many of Germany's opponents during this stretch were vastly inferior to them in skill level, that kind of goal difference is still remarkable.

And this year, Germany has achieved a balance between experience and youth. Nadine Angerer is not coming back for this World Cup, and while a tournament-long blanking is probably not in the cards again, new keeper Almuth Schult has helped Germany maintain a dominant presence between the posts. Other players, like Alexandra Popp and

Dzsenifer Marozsán (critical members of the 2015 World Cup team), will provide a strong counterpoint and stabilizing force to the raw talent present in so many of Germany's younger players.

One issue that could cause them some problems this year is a surprising lack of team coherence, which showed at various

German soccer fans expect that their women's team will give them a lot to celebrate in 2019.

times in the run-up to 2019 qualifying. All successful German squads are dedicated to a team-oriented approach that doesn't put one player over another. However, there have been occasional instances of sloppiness from the team and a me-first attitude from a few of the younger players.

Germany is also going through a transition period. Manager Steffi Jones was fired after a disappointing start to the 2018 season. Former German midfielder and Swiss national team manager Martina Voss-Tecklenburg took over in September of that year. Voss-Tecklenburg is known for improving Switzerland's soccer team so much that they reached the round of sixteen in 2015, one of their best showings ever. She coached the Swiss to a 2019 World Cup berth before taking the helm for Germany.

With a new coach and a little bit of tough love, Germany could shape up in time for the 2019 FIFA Women's World Cup. When they play as a team, it can be hard to beat any German squad in the World Cup. So while America (even with its youth) is an early front-runner for the championship, Germany is not far behind them and could emerge as a real contender soon.

TEXT-DEPENDENT QUESTIONS:

1. Which German goalkeeper holds the record for consecutive score-free minutes in a World Cup?

2. What is the name of the group that holds the German International Camp?

3. What prize did the German team earn for winning the 1989 Women's European Championship?

RESEARCH PROJECT:

Research the origins of women's soccer in Germany, including when the teams started competing, what groups control soccer, and the structure of their competitive leagues. Compare this to what you find in America and contrast the different approaches.

WORDS TO UNDERSTAND

acumen
keenness and depth of perception, discernment, or discrimination, especially in practical matters

consummate
extremely skilled and accomplished

obligatory
mandatory, required

unsurpassable
impossible to beat

CHAPTER 3

Japan

Japan's women's team is an outlier in the world of Asian soccer. It is currently the only non-European or American team to ever win the World Cup title and is one of only a handful of teams to have been present at every World Cup tournament. Its 2011 championship win over the United States made Japan just the fourth country ever to win a FIFA Women's World Cup title.

This increase in competitiveness came after a period when Japanese female soccer had almost fallen into irrelevancy. During the mid-to-late 1990s, the national team started to decline, and even failed to qualify for the 2000 Summer Olympics. This had a devastating effect on the popularity of the women's sport in Japan, and several teams in the country's Women's Football League (the L. League) folded. Things seemed hopeless until the hiring of coach Eiji Ueda turned the national team around.

Nahomi Kawasumi of Japan attempts to block a kick by American Lauren Cheney during the gold medal match at the 2012 Olympic games.

Now, Japan is considered one of the **consummate** female soccer teams in the world. Its 2011 win and second place finish at the 2015 Women's World Cup show that Japan is a force to be reckoned with and a team to watch out for in 2019.

2011 FIFA WOMEN'S WORLD CUP

The highest point of Japan's success is undoubtedly the 2011 FIFA Women's World Cup championship. That's because that win was about more than just winning some soccer games. The Japanese wanted to prove that Asian countries could compete with tough European and American teams. More importantly, it was a time for residents to celebrate after the devastation that 2011 brought to much of the country.

Earlier that year, an earthquake measuring 9.0 on the Richter scale rocked the country. The quake was the most powerful ever to hit Japan and originated just off the coast of the country. This area was the worst-possible position for it to begin, as it triggered tsunamis that devastated the coast and created waves that traveled as far as six miles inland.

In 2011, a massive earthquake off the northeast coast of Japan caused tsunamis that devastated large parts of the country, like the city of Fukushima.

Even worse, the waves caused multiple nuclear accidents across the nation. The worst occurred at the Fukushima Daiichi Nuclear Power Plant. It was there that all three reactors experienced level seven meltdowns, the worst possible outcome. Residents that lived within a twelve-mile radius of the power plant were forced to flee. By the time the damage was calculated, the country had suffered $235 billion in losses.

With all the problems back home, Japan's players had a lot on their minds when they arrived in Germany that year. They struggled through the group stage, just beating New Zealand 2–1 and then handling Mexico 4–0 before falling 2–0 to England. They then had to face an incredibly tough match against Germany in the quarterfinals. The Germans were the reigning champs and had won two times in a row.

Most experts expected the home team to sweep past the Japanese with ease, but the team-oriented defense of both sides forced a 0–0 draw in regulation time. The Germans had mostly been the aggressors during the match, but were uncharacteristically held goalless. The game went on to extra time, and in the second extra period, substitute Karina Maruyama was put into the match.

Nahomi Kawasumi catches her breath during a match against Sweden at the 2011 FIFA Women's World Cup.

As Maruyama came up the field in the 108th minute, German fans jeered her in an attempt to throw off her shot. It didn't work, however, as she blew the ball past Nadine Angerer, the keeper who had kept Germany from suffering a single goal the previous World Cup. It was just the fourth goal she had given up in the World Cup since 2007, but was the costliest one of her career. Japan held on for the 1–0 win.

Japan then easily breezed past Sweden 3–1 in the semifinals to face the United States in the final. The American team had legendary players Abby Wambach and Hope Solo leading the way this tournament and were, by far, heavy favorites over Japan. Once the Japanese beat

Germany, most people assumed the United States would easily win the whole thing.

Both teams had a lot to prove in the final. America hadn't reached the final in twelve years and wanted to win its third championship to reclaim its best in the world status. Japan, which was just the second Asian country to ever reach the final, wanted not only to prove the competitive nature of Asian soccer but also needed to bring their beleaguered home country some joy.

In spite of the United States being such heavy favorites, Japan put up an incredible fight. The defensive acumen and team-oriented approach of the Japanese consistently shut down the aggressive American offense and kept them without a goal until the sixty-ninth minute, when Alex Morgan netted a shot. With just twenty minutes left to play in the match, there was a good chance the Americans would win.

Midfielder Aya Miyama scored with nine minutes remaining to force extra time in the 2011 FIFA Women's World Cup final against the USA.

However, Aya Miyama scored the equalizer in the eighth minute to force extra time. Abby Wambach then seemed to put the dagger in Japan's chances of victory with a goal at 104 minutes, but Japanese star Homare Sawa scored an incredible goal in the 117th minute with time just about up to force a shoot-out against the United States.

Before this World Cup final, America had been excellent in shoot-out scenarios. In fact, they had won the 1999 championship in a 5–4 shoot-out after playing China to a 0–0 draw. However, their shooting was off against Japan as they fell 3–1 to give Japan its first (and so far only) World Cup championship.

JAPAN'S FINEST PLAYERS

HOMARE SAWA

Any list of Japan's **unsurpassable** soccer players needs to start with Homare Sawa. She was Japan's most important and aggressive midfielder during its 2011 and 2015 campaigns and is not only a legend in her home country, but also around the world. Her aggressive playing style and effortless scoring capabilities belie her tiny stature of 5 feet 4 inches (1.63 meters).

Sawa's skills were apparent at a very young age, as she was already playing in Japan's first division (their largest amateur league) by the age of twelve. Success continued to come quickly, as she joined the pro team Yomiuri SC Ladies Beleza at just thirteen years old and contributed seventy-nine goals in 136 matches over eight seasons. By the time she was fifteen, she was already on the national team and scored four goals in her debut match against a tough Philippines team.

The great Japanese midfielder Homare Sawa is considered to be one of the best players of her era. The longtime team captain was named FIFA Women's World Player of the Year in 2011.

Her early success meant that Sawa was an easy pick for the Japanese national team for the 1995 FIFA Women's World Cup. Before their 2011 victory, the quarterfinal exit from the 1995 tournament was Japan's best showing. In spite of failing to leave the group stages in the next three World Cups, Sawa continued to be a persistent and robust presence for the team.

Japan's surprise championship in 2011 was heavily owed to Sawa's play-making skills. For example, she scored five critical goals throughout the tournament to win the Golden Boot, including the final goal to force the championship-winning shoot-out. In fact, that goal earned Sawa a record in the Guinness book, as she scored the latest goal in

World Cup history when she tied the match in the 117th minute. Sawa won the Golden Ball as best player at the 2011 tournament.

While her team lost in a 5–2 rout to the United States in the 2015 final match, Sawa earned another spot in the Guinness records by having competed in five World Cups. Four other players, including Kristine Lilly, Bente Nordby, Miraildes Maciel Mota, and Birgit Prinz currently share this record. Sawa retired after the 2015 tournament.

YŪKI NAGASATO

Though Sawa got most of the attention during Japan's 2011 and 2015 World Cups, striker Yūki Nagasato was quietly one of the best players on the team. She is known not only for her skills, but also her persistence and intelligence on and off the pitch. In fact, she was already playing the piano and mastering the Japanese abacus at an early age in elementary school.

Yūki Nagasato [R] playing for FFC Frankfurt in the Frauen-Bundesliga. Nagasato had difficulty adjusting to life off the field in Germany due to the language barrier.

However, Nagasato fell in love with soccer and grew up playing in local youth leagues, eventually making her professional debut in Japan's L. League for Nippon TV Beleza at age fourteen. Her national team debut came two years later in an Olympic qualifying match against Thailand.

Nagasato made a move to the German league in 2010. The physicality of that team gave her an insight into what the Japanese team was missing. While the precision-based playing style of the Japanese was highly respected for its efficiency and accuracy, Nagasato knew that tougher and rougher teams were likely to continue bullying them on the field.

While Nagasato's time in Germany was difficult due to the language barrier, she learned how to read her teammates' body language and started emulating their playing styles. After three seasons, she was the team's top scorer and had mastered not only the German language, but also their physical style of play as well. When it came time to compete in the 2011 World Cup, Nagasato brought that physicality to her game.

Her combination of high soccer IQ, precision, scoring touch, and toughness made Nagasato an **obligatory** starter for the Japanese team. In 2012, she led Japan with three goals at the Olympic games in London, but the United States avenged its loss at the 2011 World Cup by beating Japan in the gold medal match 2–1. Nagasato retired from international play in 2016, but is still an active club player in the NWSL. Only Sawa, with eighty-three goals, has scored more in the history of the women's team than Nagasato, who has a total of fifty-eight.

SOCCER, MANGA, AND ANIME

Manga (comics) and anime (cartoons and movies) are very popular throughout Japan. In fact, the 2011 Women's World Cup championship team inspired a glut of manga and anime series. For those who have never watched or read these forms of Japanese entertainment, they typically feature exaggerated and cartoon-like artwork and outlandish premises, including aliens and monsters. Even tame and real-world scenarios, such as those about soccer, may highlight love triangles and complex soap-opera-level plots.

YOUTH SOCCER IN JAPAN

The most significant contributing factor to Japan's increasing success in the World Cup is its increased focus on young players. The thirty-two-team L. League started in 1989 and inspired parents and youth coaches to get more serious about the women's game.

Cultural differences, however, have made youth soccer a challenge for many players to manage. That's because most Japanese parents focus heavily on education and academic success. Sports, while not frowned upon, are not considered as important as they are in America. Therefore, the new emergence of high-quality youth leagues created a bit of friction in the nation. However, the 2011 and 2015 FIFA Women's World Cup successes have changed the attitudes of many parents and professionals.

One cultural influence on Japanese youth leagues is the emphasis on teamwork, which means that they are not committed to promoting superstar players, but rather to maximizing the success of a team. While players like Sawa and Nagasato do emerge from Japan's youth scene, most players are dedicated to finding their role on a team and perfecting it. So while there are rarely superstars, there are diverse and skilled team players. That's one reason why we're seeing an increase in Japanese players being recruited to both European and American leagues.

High-quality youth leagues are new to Japan, and they give girls an opportunity to not only learn the sport, but to develop their skills as well.

Historically Japan's youth leagues have been poorly funded, which forced a majority of teams to play on dirt fields, rather than grass. Interestingly, this has helped to make Japanese players some of the most skilled ball controllers in the world. That's because the soil on which they play and practice causes the ball to bounce in less predictable ways than it would bounce on grass. This unpredictable nature forces dedicated players to increase their ball control skills.

This lack of funding has also created what many have called a "sincere" style of Japanese soccer. Young players are not only playing on dirt fields at a young age, but also learning to take care of those fields. For example, a team coming together to drain a dirt field after a rainstorm is a widespread occurrence. They are also taught how to clean their equipment and keep their uniforms in great shape. As a result, they often develop a real understanding of the sport and a sense of team and community that they are dedicated to very early.

Another facet of the Japanese youth sports scene that impacts individual excellence is the lack of a sports-season system. Unlike the United States and other nations, which feature specific times when sports are practiced, Japanese youth players focus on one sport throughout the year. As a result, there are almost no multi-sport Japanese athletes. While this may mean that Japan will never have a Bo Jackson, it also means that dedicated players spend more time honing their skills than their American or European counterparts.

Watch Japan hit three penalty shots in the 2011 World Cup final to take home the championship

Just imagine how much more experience these young players get in soccer by concentrating on it all year. While American players get a few months in the summer or fall to play before they move on to another sport, Japanese players are practicing on dirt fields in the summer and fall and in gymnasiums during the winter and spring seasons. This dedication also minimizes the number of mistakes Japanese players make.

In fact, a heavy focus of youth coaching in Japan is to minimize the number of mistakes a player commits. When one does happen, a player typically gets punished. Even teammates are likely to yell at her for even the tiniest mistakes, such as making a wide shot at the goal. As a result, Japanese youth players are taught a careful, slow-paced, and calculated style of soccer that minimizes individual error as much as possible.

WILL THEY WIN IT ALL?

Japan's chances of repeating their 2011 victory are high. While the 5–2 loss to the United States in 2015 was undoubtedly disappointing for the nation, it has a lot of positives going for it. Japan is a top ten team in the world and the 2018 AFC Asian Cup champions. Japan beat Australia 1–0 in that tournament's final and is riding a high that will be hard to stop.

Japanese soccer fans have reason to be optimistic about the chances of their highly ranked women's team in 2019.

Beyond that, Japan has a balance of new players and veterans that can help offset the loss of Sawa and Nagasato. Players to watch include veteran midfielder Mizuho Sakaguchi and twenty-five-year-old forward Kumi Yokoyama.

However, there are a few things that Japanese soccer fans will have to worry about in 2019. First of all, the team's successes in both the 2011 and 2015 World Cups were due to narrow victories over tough teams. Beating tough teams in 1–0 games requires a lot of dedication and patience, but is also heavily based on luck. If Japan doesn't learn how to keep games from staying so close, they may be looking at a potential early exit.

Their narrow path to France 2019 is also a minor cause for concern. Their qualification run, while strong, was not exactly the most devastating example of soccer. Japan barely beat a poor Vietnam team in a tighter-than-expected match and then suffered a surprise 0–0 draw against South Korea that forced the team into a tough situation. A 1–1 draw against Australia secured a spot in the 2019 FIFA Women's World Cup, and the Japanese found their form and went undefeated the rest of the way.

Another challenge that could make it difficult for the Japanese team is their relatively new coach, Asako Takakura. She took over from Norio Sasaki, the mastermind who helped Japan reach the finals in consecutive World Cup tournaments. Thankfully for Japan, Takakura is a skilled former player who was actually in the first two World Cups for Japan. Most of her coaching success has focused on youth squads, which has earned her a few championships. While Takakura has been the coach for the team since 2016, her World Cup experience has been only at the U-20 level.

Despite some challenges, it is hard to imagine that Japan will face early elimination in 2019. The team may have reached a peak in 2011, but they were still skilled enough to make it back to the final against the United States in 2015. And if it weren't for Carli Lloyd's incredible early hat trick, the match would have been 2–2. It may even have ended in a shoot-out scenario—a situation Japan has proven itself in before.

A few critical facts put this Japanese team in perspective. Before the 2011 tournament, it had won just three of its thirteen World Cup matches. However, in the 2011 and 2015 World Cups, Japan won eleven out of thirteen contests, dropping only the 2015 final and an early group-stage match to England in the 2011 tournament. Clearly, the team has learned how to compete at a high level.

The Japanese women's team will have to come together in fine form to reach a third FIFA Women's World Cup final.

The Japanese team may have some growing pains and a little rebuilding to do going into the 2019 World Cup, but they are likely to remain one of the favorites for a championship. If they win, they'll be one of just three teams to have multiple FIFA Women's World Cup championships.

Text-Dependent Questions:

1. What event in 2011 made Japan's World Cup championship especially meaningful for the nation?

2. How many matches did Japan win in the World Cup before its 2011 win?

3. Which Japanese player holds two Guinness world records?

Research Project:

Learn more about the Japanese style of playing, including why they made such a jump in success in 2011. Take a look at the different players who contributed to the team before and after 2011 and highlight in which areas they improved the most over this period.

 WORDS TO UNDERSTAND

differential
difference between two numbers

explicitly
clearly and without any vagueness or ambiguity

multitude
many and diverse

trouncing
defeating decisively

CHAPTER 4

Norway

Nordic soccer has always had strong teams, such as Sweden and Denmark, but the strongest teams were those fielded by Norway in the first two FIFA Women's World Cup tournaments. These were the tournaments in which the Norwegians were able to nearly upset the Americans for the first World Cup championship and was followed by showcasing one of the most dominant performances in Women's World Cup history.

Since then, Norway has been a competitive team, but not a dominant one. It has had two fourth place finishes since the championship and a quarterfinal appearance. However, it didn't leave the group stage in 2011 and made it to just the round of sixteen in 2015. Norway could, however, surprise everyone in 2019 by making a turnaround for a deep run to the final. At its best, the Norwegian team is all about surprises.

NORWAY'S SUSTAINED SUCCESS

1991: SETTING THE TABLE

The future success of Norway on the world stage was set up by their progress in the 1991 FIFA Women's World Cup. The achievements in this tournament, however, were slow to build. In fact, 1991 started with a 4–0 loss to China that could have threatened Norway's chances of getting out of the group stage.

However, Norway rebounded by beating New Zealand 4–0 in its next match and then squeaked by Denmark 2–1. This result gave them four points, which was enough to come out of the group in second place. In the quarterfinal match, Norway beat Italy in a 3–2 squeaker that could have gone either way.

The Norwegians then came out strongly against Sweden, which had just won a 1–0 squeaker of its own against China, by winning 4–1. That set up the final against the United States, a team that had won its group-stage games

Elise Thorsnes of Norway [R] battles for the ball in a match against the Netherlands at UEFA Women's Euro 2017.

by outscoring opponents 11–2, and then blasted through the quarterfinals and semifinals by beating Chinese Taipei and Germany by a combined 12–2.

As a result, it was fair to say that the United States was a heavy favorite against Norway. Unlike the Norwegian team, the USWNT had steamrolled through the tournament. Therefore, few people were willing to back Norway and assumed America would blow them out. However, that ignored the fact that Norway was clearly peaking in the quarterfinals and semifinals and coming together as a tight and skilled defensive unit.

Therefore, it should not have been a shock that the final was a competitive 2–1 match. Norway easily could have won or forced a tie. The match's first goal came, unsurprisingly, from American star Michelle Akers in the twentieth minute. It was a relief for the American team because it was having a hard time getting around the Norwegian defensive pressure.

That pressure became a real problem when Norway's Linda Medalen scored nine minutes after Akers to tie the match up. For a majority of the match, there was nothing the United States could do to score. On the contrary, there were several close calls on the U.S. side, as American keeper Briana Scurry had to perform some nearly impossible saves to keep America alive. Unfortunately for the Norwegians, Akers proved her legendary status by blasting another goal past Norwegian keeper Reidun Seth with just two minutes left to play. It was a disappointing loss, but one they used as a springboard to future glory.

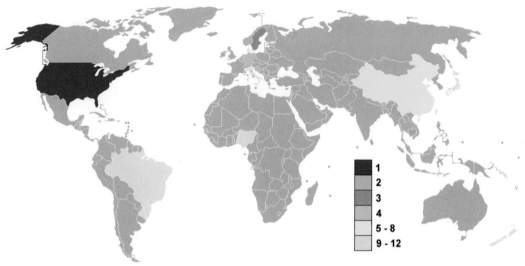

1
2
3
4
5 - 8
9 - 12

This map indicating the order of finish for the sixteen teams at the inaugural FIFA Women's World Cup in 1991 shows that Norway finished second to the United States.

THE 1995 MASTERPIECE

Norway's development as a soccer team reached a peak in 1995. After a runner-up showing at the 1991 FIFA Women's World Cup tournament, they were looking to break through as the primary Nordic female soccer power. While Sweden and Denmark had lengthier soccer histories than Norway, sustained success in a multitude of areas made the Norwegian team one of the best.

Norway was also hoping to make a name for Nordic teams after the early success of America on the world stage. The USWNT had

PERFECT TIMING

The Norwegian Women's National Team is poised to make a return to the glory it knew in the 1990s. The team moved up the FIFA rankings to number 13 in advance of the 2019 FIFA Women's World Cup, and is surging at the right time. Norway won Group 3 in UEFA Women's World Cup qualifying behind some standout performances. The team, however, would certainly be better with one key addition.

15

7 GOALS SCORED in UEFA Group 3 qualifying

LISA-MARIE KARLSENG UTLAND, FORWARD

- 26 years old
- Born in Mo i Rana, Norway
- National team debut in 2015

10

6 GOALS SCORED in UEFA Group 3 qualifying

CAROLINE GRAHAM HANSEN, MIDFIELDER

- 24 years old
- Born in Oslo, Norway
- National team debut in 2011

Ingrid Hjelmseth, Goalkeeper

- 39 years old
- Born in Lørenskog, Norway
- National team debut in 2003

01

4 CLEAN SHEETS in UEFA Group 3 qualifying

What if Norway gets its best player back - a weapon who missed the 2018 season in a dispute with the national federation **?**

2018 FIFA Best Women's Player Nominee, Ada Hegerberg, Striker

- 24 years old
- Born in Molde, Norway
- National team debut in 2011

14

38 INTERNATIONAL GOALS

beaten Norway in the first World Cup in 1991. And since Norway was playing on Swedish soil in the 1995 event, it wanted to make a point.

Norway came out strong in the 1995 group stage. The first match was an 8–0 trouncing of Nigeria that led to a surprise 2–0 blanking of England. After that win, Norway went on to blow out Canada with a 7–0 win. The incredible goal differential of plus seventeen in the group stage is one of the best in Women's World Cup history.

The knockout stage proved to be an interesting one for the team, as it faced off against Denmark in the quarterfinals. Denmark did manage to score a goal, but Norway moved smoothly past them 3–1 to set up a rematch against the United States in the semifinals. America came at the Norwegians with all-time greats like Mia Hamm and Michelle Akers, but they couldn't net a single goal.

In fact, the only score in the match came when Ann Kristin Aarønes put a goal past legendary American keeper Briana Scurry in the tenth minute of play. The rest of the match was an attempt by America to tie it up while Norway buckled down on the offensively gifted American team. The German team blanked China 1–0 in its semifinal match and moved on to play Norway for the championship.

The 1995 FIFA Women's World Cup map shows Norway with the champion's colors and Germany as runner-up.

The final against Germany was a 2–0 affair that again featured the Norwegians scoring early. They took a 1–0 lead thirty-seven minutes into the match with a goal from Hege Riise. Marianne Pettersen then netted another goal just two minutes later to give the Norwegians a lead the Germans never threatened. A considerable part of this success was due to the heroic goalkeeping of Bente Nordby.

Nordby gave up just one goal in the whole tournament, which allowed her team to accomplish a 23–1 goal record. That's an average win of about 4–0 during its six games. That kind of margin is almost unheard of in the Women's World Cup and made this Norwegian team one of the most legendary of all time. There are some who claim that they are still the best squad ever to suit up for the World Cup.

FROM FIELD TO SIDELINE

Many female soccer players have careers that last until they are in their early-to-mid thirties, though some push their bodies up to forty. These short careers are because most players start in their teens and soccer is a physically demanding sport. By the time a player reaches her mid-thirties, her reaction time is decreasing and making it harder for her to compete. However, many former players find ways to stay in their sport. Some get into coaching. Others, like the legendary Hege Riise from Norway, transition to training positions. In fact, Riise even landed a gig as assistant trainer to the U.S. Women's National Team.

BEST PLAYERS
HEGE RIISE

Hege Riise is one of Norway's most successful and respected players of all time. Her skills helped her get chosen for the national team in 1990 at age twenty-one. Without Riise and her steady hand, it's safe to say that it would have been far more challenging for Norway to make it to the finals in two consecutive World Cups, and that it would have had a minimal chance of winning the championship in 1995.

Riise was so dominant that year (along with the rest of Norway) that she not only won the Golden Ball award for the best overall player in the tournament, but also the Silver Boot award for scoring five goals as well. Norway's dominance was so complete that year that its players also won the Silver Ball (Gro Espeseth), the Bronze Ball (Ann Kristin Aarønes), and the Golden Boot (Aarønes scored six goals).

After these successes, Riise went on to help Norway through two more World Cups and two Olympic games. The Norwegians won the gold medal at the 2000 Sydney games. Riise retired in 2006 with more caps than any player in Norway's history, man or woman, at 188. Since then, she has promoted youth soccer in her home country and has worked in various training positions throughout the world. In 2003 Riise was named the best female player in Norway's history by her country's governing body.

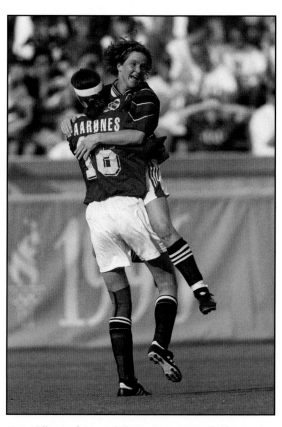

Hege Riise and Ann Kristin Aarønes were the best players on Norway's outstanding teams of the 1990s, and two of the best ever to wear Norway colors.

ANN KRISTIN AARØNES

Though Aarønes may not get the same kind of acknowledgment as Riise, she was just as crucial for their 1995 World Cup win. Her six-goal performance made her one of the top scorers in a single tournament, while her steady feet and calmness under pressure made her one of the most respected and skilled players at the forward position.

Aarønes only appeared in one more World Cup, in 1999. Her four goals in that tournament were the best for the team once again. Aarønes helped Norway power through the group stages and the quarterfinals with a 16–3 goal record and helped the team look ready to repeat their success. However, it failed to score for the rest of the event, falling 5–0 to China and then losing a shoot-out 5–4 after a goalless third place match.

In spite of that setback, Aarønes helped her team win a bronze medal at the 1996 Atlanta Olympic games and was chosen for the all-star team in 1999 for her contributions to her team's success. After that, she signed with the Women's United Soccer Association in 2001 for one season before retiring from the sport. Her sixty international goals are third all-time in Norway's history.

ADA HEGERBERG

When it comes to modern Norwegian players, few are as dominating as striker Ada Hegerberg. In fact, if Norway wants to return to the glory of 1995, it will be on the back of this player. At just twenty-four years old, she is already known as one of the deadliest scorers of her generation. Somehow, she already has more than 250 total goals to her name. With fewer than seventy caps, she took over eighth place on the all-time Norwegian women's goal scoring list. Hegerberg is likely to make a significant impression at the 2019 World Cup.

In 2015, Ada Hegerberg became the first woman to win the Norwegian Golden Ball as the best soccer player in the country of either sex since the great Hege Riise in 1995.

Her raw talent and potential make Hegerberg a natural choice for this list. For example, she scored three goals in seven minutes while playing for Norwegian team Kolbotn

Ada Hegerberg talks about her nomination for Women's Player of the Year

to earn one of the quickest hat tricks ever for the team. In her debut World Cup tournament in 2015, she scored three goals in three group-stage matches on a youthful team packed with potential.

That success helped Hegerberg earn the 2015 Norwegian Golden Ball, an award that is given out to the best player in the country. For twenty years, it had been given out to men. Can you guess the last female winner? Hege Riise, of course, who was rewarded for her incredible contributions to the 1995 World Cup win.

NORWAY'S YOUTH LEAGUES

Norway's youth leagues are very competitive and set up in a way that encourages competition and professional scouting. Teams can be started by anybody who is willing to pay a small registration fee and who can find a league that wants to add to its roster of teams. As a result, there are now more than 1,400 different youth teams throughout the nation at a variety of different age levels. The tiers of these teams include everything from Under-11s to Under-19s.

Soccer is commonly played in the schools of the country, but many of these youth leagues are explicitly designed as skill-training groups that all build up to what is known as the Norway Cup. This youth competition is, by far, the most significant and most crucial youth event for Norwegian soccer players and, in some instances, even players from other European nations. This event includes matches for all tiers of youth soccer for both male and female players.

The scope of the event is almost impossible to grasp for many American readers. There will be 1,400 different teams across the different age tiers competing to be the best team. More than a dozen venues are packed with players, clubs, and spectators throughout the event. There are usually more than 30,000 different players involved and often just as many (if not more) attendees. A further 400 participants take the form of referees, and they come from all across the world.

What is particularly interesting about this event is that while it is mostly Norwegian teams competing for the duration of the event, foreign groups are welcome to compete. Therefore, you might see a Dutch team competing against one from England, or even America. During the event, all of the finals are broadcast on television to increasing national and international interest. One Norwegian newspaper, *Dagbladet*, uses several of its sports pages covering this event every year.

As a result, this event is a significant scouting opportunity for various soccer leagues around the nation, and even the world. The professional association in Norway, which includes a pyramid structure similar to English soccer, often picks many local players. This includes teams at multiple divisions that compete to rise to more difficult (and higher-paying) leagues, and to avoid falling to a lower one.

Crowds begin to arrive for the day's activities at the Norway Cup, a massive youth soccer competition in a suburb of Oslo.

However, there are also chances for skilled youth players to get picked up by American and European leagues, or to even get chosen for the Norwegian national team. This system has helped to streamline the selection process for the country and has become an efficient way of getting the best players onto Norway's Olympic and World Cup teams, both male and female.

CAN THEY DO IT AGAIN?

Norway's path to a championship in 2019 might seem pretty steep to the casual fan. After all, they failed to get out of the group stage in 2011 after barely beating Equatorial Guinea in a 1–0 game and then losing 3–0 against Brazil and 2–1 against Australia. Norway didn't advance past the round of sixteen (in the newly expanded twenty-four-team tournament) in 2015, but they had a much better showing.

For example, their group stage was highlighted by a 4–0 win over Thailand and a 3–1 win over Ivory Coast. They also drew against Germany 1–1 and scored seven points to tie Germany and advance to the knockout stage. A match against England in the round of sixteen awaited.

It looked pretty good for Norway early on, as Solveig Gulbrandsen scored just nine minutes into the match with a flawless header. Unfortunately for the Norwegians, England's Steph Houghton scored seven minutes later to even it up and then took the lead on a Lucy Bronze goal to knock Norway out of the tournament once again.

So while that early exit was a difficult defeat for the Norwegians, there is a good chance they could go further in 2019. It will be a challenge if Hegerberg, who left the team in 2017 in a dispute with Norway's soccer federation, does not participate. However,

Norwegian defender and captain Maren Mjelde (L) will need to be at the top of her game to have a chance of leading her team on a deep World Cup run in 2019.

experienced players like captain Maren Mjelde and goalkeeper Ingrid Hjelmseth are both at the peak of skill level and maturity. These skills will be necessary for allowing scorers like Isabell Herlovsen and Caroline Graham Hansen the chance to do their thing in a devastating way.

Norway is not as highly ranked by FIFA as some of the bigger favorites, but it is in the top fifteen and has the pieces in place to break out of its post-95 World Cup rut to emerge as one of the most dominant and impressive teams in the sport. Whether or not it regains the championship remains to be seen, but don't be surprised if you see them making their deepest run in more than a decade.

Text-Dependent Questions:

1. In what year did Norway win the World Cup?

2. Which keeper recorded a 23–1 goal record for Norway?

3. Where did Norway place in the 2015 Women's World Cup?

Research Project:

Do some research on team Norway's current training program to learn more about how it plans on overcoming its recent World Cup struggles. Discuss not only the dietary plans, but also the kinds of exercises the players are performing to improve their chances.

 WORDS TO UNDERSTAND

aplomb
complete self-confidence or assurance

demoralizing
weakening the morale of someone

potent
having great power, influence, or effect

unnerving
upsetting, intimidating

CHAPTER 5

Best of the Rest

The teams highlighted in the previous chapters are among the best in the world, but they are not alone at the top. In fact, there are four other teams that are considered real threats for the 2019 FIFA Women's World Cup championship. Let's take a brief look at all four and gauge their chances of success.

SWEDEN REMAINS CONSISTENT

Sweden's women's World Cup tournaments have been exciting, and sometimes rocky, experiences that have nonetheless shown that it is one of the best teams in the world. Like its neighbor Norway, Sweden has qualified for every World Cup appearance. Unlike Norway, however, it has yet to win a championship. The closest opportunity came in 2003 when Sweden was the runner-up.

Since that time, Sweden earned a third place finish in 2011 but struggled in 2007 and 2015. In the first year, it didn't advance out of the group stage and failed to get out of the new round of sixteen in 2015. Sweden's active youth soccer program has helped it remain an international presence.

Sweden lost to Japan in the semifinals of the 2011 FIFA Women's World Cup.

OH SO CLOSE

Entering the 2003 FIFA Women's World Cup, Sweden had picked up a third place finish and two quarterfinal appearances in previous World Cups. This success made them a team that needed to be watched. Group-stage success was surprisingly modest in 2003, as Sweden won two and lost one and had a goal record of just 5–3. The only goals it gave up were in a 3–1 loss to the United States, as Sweden blanked North Korea 1–0 and Nigeria 3–0.

Then the Swedes took advantage of several close calls to advance through the quarterfinals and semifinals. Their first win came against Brazil, where they held out defensively for a 2–1 win. This success came in spite of the presence of Brazil's Marta, a player who is often considered the best in the world. Sweden then overcame an increasingly confident Canadian team 2–1 before falling to Germany 2–1 in the final.

A considerable part of this achievement came from Victoria Svensson, who can rightfully be called one of Sweden's best players of all time. She won awards for top Swedish soccer player in 1998 and 2003 and retired with 166 caps and sixty-eight goals. Hanna Ljungberg was also a critical player, as she scored three goals across the tournament in what were always tight games. Her career ended in 2008 with 130 caps and seventy-two goals.

DOES SWEDEN HAVE A CHANCE OF WINNING?

Sweden is one of only a handful of countries to qualify for every World Cup tournament since its debut. Its opponents also consider it one of the most dangerous and consistent teams. Sweden's strong youth program selects the best players every year and gets them into training camps as quickly as possible. In this way, they can cherry-pick the best players for the national team.

This smart move has developed some of the best names in Swedish soccer, including midfielder Kosovare Asllani, a player who earned four goals in Sweden's 2019 qualification run. Another high-quality player to watch in 2019 is twenty-three-year-old forward Stina Blackstenius, who added another three goals. Captain Caroline Seger and defender Nilla Fischer are also likely to be demoralizing to any team playing against Sweden this year.

One of the top defenders in the world, Sweden's Nilla Fischer will anchor the team's back line during France 2019.

Sweden's style of play is more often highlighted by a cohesive team strategy rather than by superstar players. This fact is critical to consider, because one mistake could throw the whole system for a loop. However, few teams are as deadly as Sweden when it gets locked into a groove, so expect good things in 2019.

BRAZIL COULD MAKE ITS BIG BREAK

Soccer is always a big deal in Brazil, no matter if it is the men's or women's team. Unfortunately, the women's team has yet to bring home the World Cup trophy. Its best showings were a 2007 runner-up appearance against a dominant German team and a third place finish in 1999.

Brazil has also reached the quarterfinals twice for fifth place finishes and have been in ninth place three other times, including as recently

WORLD CUP RESULTS

 1991

 1995

 1999

 2003

WINNER USA	WINNER NORWAY	WINNER USA	WINNER GERMANY
RUNNER-UP Norway	RUNNER-UP Germany	RUNNER-UP China	RUNNER-UP Sweden

2007

2011

2015

2019

WINNER GERMANY

WINNER JAPAN

WINNER USA

France has never finished higher than 4th (2011), but the hosts will be one of the favorites to win in 2019

RUNNER-UP
Brazil

RUNNER-UP
USA

RUNNER-UP
Japan

as 2015. While this might not seem like the resume of the most **potent** team on the list, there is one player that always makes Brazil a real World Cup threat.

MARTA ALWAYS GIVES BRAZIL A REAL CHANCE

If you've never heard of Marta, 2019 is an excellent time to start paying attention to Brazil. This skilled player is often considered the best female player of all time and is already a living legend in her home country.

Any team with five-time FIFA Women's Player of the Year award winner Marta has to be taken seriously.

Between 2006 and 2010, she was awarded FIFA Women's World Player of the Year honors a record five straight times. Marta was both the Golden Shoe and the Golden Ball winner in the 2007 World Cup during a tournament in which she scored seven goals. With a career scoring average just shy of one goal per match in international appearances, she is a force of nature in the sport. At thirty three years old, 2019 might well be her last chance to will her team to a World Cup title.

The 2007 World Cup seemed predestined to be a Germany and Brazil final. Marta and her squad breezed through the group stage by outscoring their opponents 10–0. They beat New Zealand 5–0, Denmark 1–0, and surprised China with a 4–0 blanking. However, the path to the semifinals just about came to an end in the quarterfinals against Australia.

This 3–2 win for Brazil started out well when it scored a goal in the first five minutes of the match. They then went up 2–0 when Marta netted a penalty kick. However, Australia tied things up with goals in the thirty-sixth and sixty-eighth minutes, setting up late-game heroics from Cristiane Rozeira, another incredible Brazilian player who has more than eighty goals in a fifteen-year career. Cristiane scored the match winner with fifteen minutes remaining. However, the unforgettable performance from Germany's goalkeeper Nadine Angerer in the final kept Brazil goalless in a 2–0 loss.

IS THIS BRAZIL'S YEAR?

When your team has a player like 2018 Best FIFA Women's Player award winner Marta on it, you are always going to be a competitive powerhouse. Unfortunately, Brazil has yet to match its 2007 performance at the World Cup. However, there is no reason why it couldn't achieve real success this year. For example, Cristiane will be back to provide her teammates with a steadying presence and another scoring threat.

While there are always heartaches and unexpected wins and losses every World Cup, it does feel like Brazil is due a championship this year. With

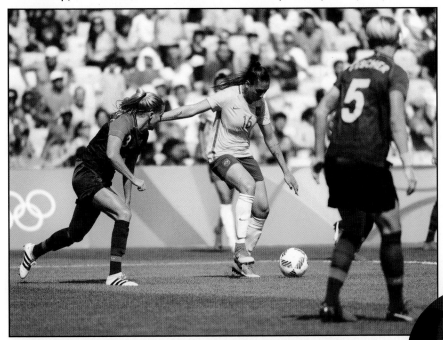

Beatriz is part of the strong supporting cast around Marta that will give Brazil a chance to win in France.

skilled coaching and the athletic abilities of two of the sport's best goal scorers, we can expect Brazil to be a challenge against whomever they play.

BRAZIL'S LENGTHY HISTORY OF SOCCER

Few nations, including most in Europe, have such an intense love affair with soccer that Brazil has. The first official soccer match in the country was played in 1894 after a man named Thomas Donohue introduced the sport to the nation. This Scottish-born man had been teaching the Brazilian natives soccer for a few years, and fellow Scotsman Charles Miller set up the country's first league at the turn of the last century. However, there were other instances of soccer popping up across the nation as early as the 1870s, including along the burgeoning railroad systems that crisscrossed the country. As a result of this early introduction, the country is a significant soccer stronghold and has innovated many offensive and defensive concepts.

CHINESE THREAT

In 1999, China was the runner-up against a dominant American team and have since never finished higher than the quarterfinals. However, the Chinese team has remained one of the most **unnerving** teams in World Cup history. They play an exact and calculating game that requires a lot of patience to beat.

1999 FIFA WOMEN'S WORLD CUP

China's best chance at winning the World Cup came in 1999 when superstar forward Sun Wen was in her prime. Wen is not only China's best player ever, but also could be one of the top two or three players ever in the world. In fact, fans voted Wen FIFA Female Player of the Century in 2002 (Michelle Akers from the United States won the FIFA Football Committee vote).

The group stage went well for the Chinese against both good and bad teams. They won 2–1 against the always-challenging Swedish squad and then stomped poor Ghana 7–0. After that, they beat Australia 3–1 to finish with a 12–2 goal spread and a first place finish in the group. Five of those goals belonged to Wen.

The knockout stage was almost as easy for Wen and her teammates. They beat Russia 2–0 in the quarterfinals and blew past Norway 5–0 in the semifinals. Two of those goals belonged to Wen as she continued to be an active on-field general for her teammates. The final against America was a tough match against a great team in its home country.

Sun Wen is the best player in the history of Chinese women's soccer, and one of the greatest ever to play. She was named co-winner of the FIFA Female Player of the Century award in 2002.

With aplomb, Wen and the rest of her squad just about pulled off the ultimate upset. The ordinarily offensively-dominant U.S. team couldn't get anything past keeper Gao Hung. America's keeper Briana Scurry was just as good between the posts, forcing a 0–0 draw that was not broken in extra time.

During the shoot-out, the Chinese and Americans went shot-for-shot with each other, but America edged them out in a dramatic 5–4 finish. Wen won both the Golden Ball and the Golden Boot, while China received the Fair Play award for the clean play that drew very few penalties throughout the tournament.

IS CHINA A REAL CONTENDER?

Losing a once-in-a-lifetime player like Wen is always going to challenge any team. China was no different, as it has struggled to regain its footing after Wen's retirement in 2006. The low point came in 2011 when the Chinese failed to qualify for the tournament for the first time in team history.

However, they may be in a better place than they have been in quite a few years.

Li Ying's strong qualifying tournament bodes well for a good performance at the 2019 FIFA Women's World Cup.

For example, their qualification for 2019 was quite simple. After beating Thailand 4–0 in the opener to the 2018 AFC Women's Asian Cup, China swept the Philippines 3–0 and crushed Jordan 8–1 to become the first team to qualify for the tournament. These strong showings indicate that Chinese soccer may be on the rebound and that it could be the year for them to do real damage, particularly with the help of Li Ying, a twenty-six-year-old midfielder who scored seven goals in the qualifying tournament. Veteran forward Ma Xiaoxu, one of the top goal scorers in team history, is always a threat.

HOST-COUNTRY BOOST

France has a mixed history in the FIFA Women's World Cup. The French failed to qualify until 2003, when they quickly exited in the group stage. Their next appearance came in 2011, when France made a splash with a fourth place finish, followed by a fifth place finish in 2015. As 2019's host country, France is bound to come in with confidence.

THE RISE OF FRANCE

It's fair to say that people didn't expect much out of France in 2011. After all, they'd only ever qualified for one World Cup before and didn't look that strong on paper. However, people who knew the team understood that it had been growing a lot over the previous few years by recruiting high-quality players.

As a result, France was able to creep out of the group stages by beating Nigeria 1–0 and Canada 4–0. The 4–2 loss to Germany seemed inevitable here, given the Germans were the two-time defending champions. Still, two wins were enough to move to the quarterfinals, where France pulled off a 4–3 shoot-out win against England after forcing a 1–1 draw through extra time.

French superstar Amandine Henry heads the ball during the 2018 UEFA Women's Champions League final. The striker must be a factor for France to win the 2019 FIFA Women's World Cup on home soil.

The semifinals were not as kind to the team, as it lost 3–1 against the United States and then 2–1 against Sweden. However, spectators were surprised and impressed by the team's defensive-oriented play and its significant improvement since the last appearance in the tournament eight years prior.

The French were even better in 2015, with players like midfielder Amandine Henry and goalkeeper Sarah Bouhaddi leading the way. These two are likely to be the pillars on which France builds its hopes in 2019. Just as these players came out of the expanding youth league sector in France, more players of their quality could be forthcoming.

Learn more about France's goalkeeper training methods by watching this video

And while France ultimately came in fifth in the 2015 tournament, that's a more significant accomplishment because the newly expanded tournament schedule forced them to play more matches. As a result, the impressive 3–0 win over South Korea in the round of sixteen can be taken as a sign of good things to come in 2019.

IS A WIN POSSIBLE?

France has continued to build on the success it enjoyed over the last two tournaments. A top five team in the FIFA rankings, it has a lot more offensive and defensive weapons than in the past. The veteran Henry is likely to remain a goal-scoring threat for the team in 2019 after winning the Silver Ball in 2015.

Bouhaddi should also retain her spot as a key weapon in France's arsenal. She gave up just two goals in the qualifying matches in 2015 before giving up only one in the quarterfinal match against Germany. Expect this seasoned pro to be a dominant force. Another of France's veteran stars, defender Wendie Renard, is also likely to make significant contributions throughout the tournament.

With all of these key figures in place, it is hard to imagine that France won't make a deep run this tournament. On paper, this is the best French side the women have ever sent to a World Cup. With the country riding high following the men's team win in 2018, the sound and fury of their home crowd cheering them on could serve as a significant inspiration for success for the women.

Text-Dependent Questions:

1. What country has a runner-up finish and two third place finishes in the World Cup?

2. Which Brazilian player scored seven goals in the 2007 World Cup?

3. What was the score of China's 1999 World Cup final game?

Research Project:

Investigate a country that qualified for the 2019 FIFA Women's World Cup that isn't getting a lot of press. Research how long it has been participating in the tournament, how it prepared, and which players could make a name for themselves in 2019.

Club: collective name for a team, and the organization that runs it.

CONCACAF: acronym for the *Confederation of North, Central American and Caribbean Association Football*, the governing body of the sport in North and Central America and the Caribbean; pronounced "kon-ka-kaff."

Extra time: additional period, normally two halves of 15 minutes, used to determine the winner in some tied cup matches.

Full-time: the end of the game, signaled by the referees whistle (also known as the *final whistle*).

Goal difference: net difference between goals scored and goals conceded. Used to differentiate league or group stage positions when clubs are tied on points.

Hat trick: when a player scores three goals in a single match.

Own-goal: where a player scores a goal against her own team, usually as the result of an error.

Penalty area: rectangular area measuring 44 yards (40.2 meters) by 18 yards (16.5 meters) in front of each goal; commonly called "the box."

Penalty kick: kick taken 12 yards (11 meters) from goal, awarded when a team commits a foul inside its own penalty area.

Penalty shootout: method of deciding a match in a knockout competition, which has ended in a draw after full-time and extra-time. Players from each side take turns to attempt to score a penalty kick against the opposition goalkeeper. Sudden death is introduced if scores are level after each side has taken five penalties.

Side: Another word for team

Stoppage time: an additional number of minutes at the end of each half, determined by the match officials, to compensate for time lost during the game. Informally known by various names, including *injury time* and *added time*.

UEFA: acronym for *Union of European Football Associations*, the governing body of the sport in Europe; pronounced "you-eh-fa."

Lloyd, Carli and Coffey, Wayne. *When Nobody Was Watching: My Hard-Fought Journey to the Top of the Soccer World*. Boston, Massachusetts: Houghton Mifflin Harcourt, 2016.

Killion, Ann. *Champions of Women's Soccer*. New York, New York: Philomel Books, 2018.

Williams, Jenn. *Globalising Women's Football: Europe, Migration, and Professionalization*. Bern, Switzerland: Peter Lang AG, 2013.

Oxenham, Gwendolyn. *Under the Lights and In the Dark: Untold Stories of Women's Soccer*. London, England: Icon Books, 2017.

Christopher, Matt. *World Cup: An Action-Packed Look at Soccer's Biggest Competition*. New York, New York: Brown Books for Young Readers, 2018.

INTERNET RESOURCES

https://www.fifa.com/womensworldcup/index.html
The English-language section of the FIFA Women's World Cup site allows you to track your favorite team's progress and to catch the latest scores.

http://www.espn.com/soccer/league/_/name/fifa.wwc
ESPN's popular site on FIFA World Cup soccer lets you track individual games and even the statistics of players and teams that you enjoy watching.

https://www.fifa.com/fifa-world-ranking/ranking-table/women/index.html
FIFA's regularly updated ranking of the various national women's teams around the world. This site includes a listing of their points and their changing positions.

https://equalizersoccer.com/
The world's best female soccer magazine includes detailed examinations of teams, updates on league play around the world, and predictions for this year's FIFA Women's World Cup tournament.

http://www.espn.com/espnw/sport/soccer/
ESPN's women soccer site lets you track a multitude of professional, amateur, and collegiate teams and read high-quality articles on a variety of subjects.

Aarønes, Ann Kristin, 54, 56–57
Advanced Youth Soccer Educational System (AYSES), 31
Akers, Michelle, 14, 50, 54, 71
    chronic fatigue syndrome, 14
American Youth Soccer Organization (AYSO), 15
Angerer, Nadine, 26, 28–29, 34, 39, 69
Argentina, 24, 26
Asllani, Kosovare, 65
Australia, 10, 45, 60, 71

Blackstenius, Stina, 65
Bouhaddi, Sarah, 74–75
Brazil, 9, 12, 14, 26, 29, 60, 64–65, 68–70
Brian, Morgan, 18, 20
Bronze, Lucy, 60
Bronze Ball, 14, 56

Canada, 24, 54, 64, 73
Chastain, Brandi, 9–10
    jersey, 10
Cheney, Lauren, 37
China, 40, 49, 57, 68, 70–72
Chinese Taipei, 50

Dahlkemper, Abby, 19
Denmark, 49, 54, 68
DiCicco, Tony, 28–29
Donohue, Thomas, 70

Elite Clubs National League, 17
Ellis, Jill, 19
England, 26, 33, 39, 54, 60, 73
Equatorial Guinea, 60
Espeseth, Gro, 56

Fair Play award, 71
Fawcett, Joy, 9
Female European Player of the Century, 29
FIFA Female Player of the Century, 70–71
FIFA Women's Player of the Year, 68
FIFA Women's World Cup
    1991, 13–14, 49–51, 66
    1995, 41, 51, 54–56, 66
    1999, 8–10, 13, 57, 66, 70–71
    2003, 20, 23–25, 33, 63, 66, 72
    2007, 20, 23, 25–28, 33, 63, 65, 67, 69
    2011, 37–46, 49, 63, 67, 72–74
    2015, 10–11, 19, 34, 38, 42, 44, 46, 49, 58, 63, 67, 74
    2019, 18–21, 33–35, 46–47, 52, 57, 60–61, 67–68, 73–75
FIFA Women's World Player, 27
Fischer, Nilla, 65
France, 67, 72–75
Frauen-Bundesliga, 28–29, 42
Fukushima Daiichi Nuclear Power Plant, 39

Germany, 9, 20–21, 23–35, 39–40, 42–43, 50, 54–55, 60, 64–69, 73
Ghana, 71
Golden Ball award, 25, 27, 42, 56–58, 68, 71
Golden Boot award, 41, 71
Golden Glove award, 11
Golden Shoe award, 68
Guinness Book of Records, 41–42
Gulbrandsen, Solveig, 60

Hamm, Mia, 12–14
    marketing deals, 13
Hansen, Caroline Graham, 52, 61
Harris, Ashlyn, 19
Hegergerg, Ada, 53, 57–58, 60
Henry, Amandine, 73–74
Herlovsen, Isabell, 61
Hingst, Ariane, 26
Hjelmseth, Ingrid, 53
Horan, Lindsey, 20
Houghton, Steph, 60
Hung, Gao, 71

International Federation of Football History & Statistics (IFFHS), 29
Ivory Coast, 33, 60

Japan, 10–11, 24, 26, 37–47, 67
    earthquake, 38–39
Johnston, Julie, 10
Jones, Steffi, 34

Kawasumi, Nahomi, 37, 39
Künzer, Nia, 25

Lavelle, Rose, 18–19
Lilly, Kristine, 42
Lingor, Renate, 26
Ljungberg, Hanna, 25, 64
Lloyd, Carli, 11, 18–19, 46

Manga and anime, 43
Marozsán, Dzsenifer, 34
Marta, 26, 29, 64, 68–69
Maruyama, Karina, 39
Medalen, Linda, 51
Meinert, Maren, 25
Mewis, Samantha, 18–19
Mexico, 39
Milbrett, Tiffany, 9
Miller, Charles, 70
Miyama, Aya, 40
Mjelde, Maren, 60–61
Mohr, Heidi, 29–30
Morgan, Alex, 20, 40
Mota, Miraildes Maciel, 42

Naeher, Alyssa, 19
Nagasato, Yūki, 10, 42–44, 46
Netherlands, 50
New Zealand, 39, 49, 68
Nigeria, 10, 54, 64, 73
Nordby, Bente, 42, 55
North Korea, 26, 64
Norway, 26, 29, 33, 49–61, 66, 71

Olympic Games, 18, 27, 56
    1996, 14, 57
    2000, 37
    2004, 14
    2012, 37, 43
Order of Merit honor, 14

Pettersen, Marianne, 55
Philippines, 72
Popp, Alexandra, 34
Press, Christen, 20
Prinz, Birgit, 25–28, 42

Rapinoe, Megan, 20
Renard, Wendie, 75
Riise, Hege, 55–56
Rozeira, Cristiane, 69
Russia, 24, 71

Sakaguchi, Mizuho, 46
Sasaki, Norio, 46
Sauerbrunn, Becky, 19
Sawa, Homare, 40–44, 46
Schächter Management Sports, 31
Schult, Almuth, 34
Scurry, Briana, 9, 51, 54, 71

Seger, Caroline, 65
Sexism, 23
Silver Ball award, 26
Silver Boot award, 29, 56
Solo, Hope, 10–11, 39
South Korea, 46, 74
Stegemann, Kerstin, 26
Svensson, Victoria, 64
Sweden, 10, 24–25, 33, 39, 49, 51, 63–65, 71, 74
Switzerland, 34

Takakura, Asako, 46
Thailand, 33, 42, 60, 72
Thorsnes, Elise, 50
TuS Niederkirchen, 29

Ueda, Eiji, 37
U.S. men's team, 15
U.S. Women's National Team (USWNT), 7–14, 18–21, 24, 26, 29, 33, 37, 39–40, 42–43, 45, 49–50, 54, 64, 66–67, 71, 74
U.S Youth Soccer, 15
Utland, Lisa-Marie Karlseng, 52

Vietnam, 46
Voss-Tecklenburg, Martina, 34

Wambach, Abby, 12, 39–40
Washington Spirit, 19
Wen, Sun, 70–72
Western New York Flash, 19
Wiegmann, Bettina, 9

Ying, Lu, 72
Yokoyama, Kumi, 46
Yomiuri SC Ladies Beleza, 41
Youth development programs
    Germany, 30–32
    Japan, 43–45
    Norway, 58–59
    Sweden, 63–64
    U.S., 15–17

AUTHOR'S BIOGRAPHY

Bryce Kane is a professional writer with over ten years of experience. For three years, he worked as a sports writer for a daily newspaper covering a multitude of sporting events, including multiple state championships. In 2009, he earned a master's degree in fiction writing and is currently working on two books while enjoying a relaxing life in Traverse City, Michigan, as a freelance writer.

EDUCATIONAL VIDEO LINKS

Chapter 1: http://x-qr.net/1EF8
Chapter 2: http://x-qr.net/1HdK
Chapter 3: http://x-qr.net/1Dva

Chapter 4: http://x-qr.net/1Hhx
Chapter 5: http://x-qr.net/1Hcq

PICTURE CREDITS